CLEVER MONKEY

Stephen Elboz

Illustrated by
Peter Bowman

OXFORD
UNIVERSITY PRESS

OXFORD
UNIVERSITY PRESS

Great Clarendon Street, Oxford OX2 6DP

Oxford University Press is a department of the University of Oxford.
It furthers the University's objective of excellence in research, scholarship,
and education by publishing worldwide in

Oxford New York

Auckland Bangkok Buenos Aires Cape Town Chennai
Dar es Salaam Delhi Hong Kong Istanbul Karachi Kolkata
Kuala Lumpur Madrid Melbourne Mexico City Mumbai Nairobi
São Paulo Shanghai Singapore Taipei Tokyo Toronto

with an associated company in Berlin

Oxford is a registered trade mark of Oxford University Press
in the UK and in certain other countries

British Library Cataloguing in Publication Data

Data available

ISBN 0 19 919498 X

3 5 7 9 10 8 6 4 2

Guided Reading Pack (6 of the same title): ISBN 0 19 919577 3
Mixed Pack (1 of 6 different titles): ISBN 0 19 919499 8
Class Pack (6 copies of 6 titles): ISBN 0 19 919500 5

Printed in Hong Kong

This book is for Shaun Dunnett

Contents

Chapter 1
The Lost Keys

My name is Sandy Longtail. I live with my Mum and Dad and Jem my sister at Monkey Land Safari Park, home of the most intelligent monkeys in the whole world. It's a nice place to live. Trouble is, nothing much ever happens here …

Then one day, exciting news reached my tree.

The head keeper, Mr Otterbank, had lost his big bunch of keys. And a monkey had found them!

An urgent meeting was called about it.

The meeting was held that night at the tree of Milton Grizzlefur, the cleverest monkey in all of Monkey Land.

He doesn't look clever though. That's because he spends all day in a tyre hanging from an old tree.

(I say it looks like he's fast asleep. "No, no," says Mum. "Not asleep. Milton Grizzlefur is thinking.")

We all stood waiting for Milton Grizzlefur to wake up – I mean, to stop thinking.

At last he opened one yellow eye.

"Ah, yes, as I was saying," he said, his grey whiskers looking a bit like a human's beard.

"You weren't saying anything at all," I thought. But I kept quiet about it.

"The keys," continued Milton Grizzlefur. "And what to do with them. Of course, we shall give them back. But the question is ... Do we do it at once, or shall we – hmm – have a little fun with them first?"

His tyre spun him round the wrong way. This gave me and the other monkeys time to think.

We all knew what Milton Grizzlefur was getting at. It was the dearest wish of every monkey there to see the world outside Monkey Land.

We knew there was a lot to see. Nearly every night, Milton Grizzlefur read out the most interesting bits from a newspaper, rescued from the rubbish bin. But although we had learned many things about the world, it was not the same as seeing it with our own eyes.

By the time the tyre had turned him back again, most monkeys had made up their mind.

Dad cleared his throat.

"Before we give Mr Otterbank his keys back, I should like to see what lies behind the big wire fence," he said. "For one night, I should like my freedom."

Monkey heads all around nodded in agreement. Oh look! Mine was nodding with them.

"But won't we need a disguise?" called Tonto Gribb, the big ginger monkey. "The humans will get nervous if they see a band of monkeys on the loose."

"That's true," added Mum. "It wouldn't be fair to get Mr Otterbank into trouble."

"Ah," said Milton Grizzlefur, "I've already thought of that. Anyone who wants to go on this little adventure, raise your paw."

Of course everyone did.

"Good, then follow me."

Chapter 2
Milton Grizzlefur's Plan

Milton Grizzlefur climbed down his
tree. And because he was so old, he
climbed slowly. He walked slowly too,
stopping now and again to sniff the air.

"I wish he'd get a move on," said
Jem. "Where do you think he's taking
us?"

"How do I know baboon face? It
looks like Mr Otterbank's house."

And so it turned out to be.

We all stood at the wire gate leading into Mr Otterbank's garden.

The house was already dark. Mr Otterbank went to bed at sundown and got up again at sunrise.

Milton Grizzlefur said, "I have been looking at Mr Otterbank's keys. This one, for example, will open this gate, here."

Click. He had opened it. And before we knew it, we had followed him into Mr Otterbank's garden.

"This one will open Mr Otterbank's front door," Milton Grizzlefur went on, holding up a different key.

"How did Mr Otterbank manage to lock it, then?" asked Stanley Woolback, looking puzzled.

"Mrs Otterbank has a spare set of keys," Milton Grizzlefur explained.

Mum raised her paw to ask another question.

"Why do we need to get into Mr Otterbank's house at all?"

"Dear Mrs Longtail," said Milton Grizzlefur. "We need to borrow some human clothes. Only for the night, you understand. We need the clothes of Mr Otterbank, Mrs Otterbank and both their children.

("Wow," I thought. "I get to wear trousers!")

"Now," continued Milton Grizzlefur.
"I need a couple of volunteers, willing
to be our burglars, so to speak."

I was so excited, I jumped up in the
air. When I came down, I landed on
Dad's tail. Then he jumped in the air.
He jumped in surprise!

Milton Grizzlefur thought we were
volunteering.

"Well done, Otis and Sandy. In you
go!"

"But ... but ... "

Poor Dad. He was still 'but ...
butting' as we were pushed through Mr
Otterbank's door and into his hallway.

"Good luck," said Milton Grizzlefur.

Chapter 3
Hunt the Clothes

Dad and I wandered through a few rooms, getting used to the dark. Neither of us made a sound with our paws.

"Dad," I whispered, "I've just had a thought. Where do humans keep their clothes?"

"How do I know?" said Dad. He was still cross about his tail. "Fur has always been good enough for me."

"What about in here?" I pulled open
a likely looking door.

A light came on. I jumped into the
air and landed on a table.

Dad sighed and gently shut the door.
"That, Sandy, is called a fridge.
Humans keep their food in it. I think
we have to look upstairs."

We went along the hall and up the stairs. These are a good invention in houses, but they wouldn't work so well in trees.

"I can hear Mr Otterbank snoring," I giggled.

"Just as long as he doesn't hear *you*," said Dad, tweaking my ear. "Now, this is called a bedroom —"

We went inside. Mr and Mrs
Otterbank were two big lumps in a bed.
Some clothes were on a chair, and we
grabbed them.

"There must be more somewhere,"
said Dad. "Look in those drawers. They
pull out, so be careful."

Soon we had a big pile of clothes
which we took out into the hallway.
Then Dad went to search in the
children's room. I opened a window
and threw out everything we had into
the garden.

Below me I heard the mutter of monkey voices, saying things like:

"Has anyone got the other shoe?"

"Do purple and orange go together?"

And, "Paws off! I saw that first."

Dad came out with the children's clothes, and he said it sounded like a real old jumble sale. Before I could ask what a jumble sale was, Dad tossed the clothes out of the window. We hurried downstairs and out of the house.

What a sight we saw.
Little humans!

That's what they looked like. Of
course, the clothes were rather large for
monkeys. (Even though Mr Otterbank
and his wife are quite small for
humans.) Everyone was busily turning
up cuffs and trousers.

I didn't recognize Mum and Jem. It
was a good job Mum called to us.

"Over here," she said. "I've saved you
some stuff."

When we were dressed, Milton Grizzlefur inspected us. He was wearing golfing pants and a cap. His ears still stuck out somewhat.

"You need to pull down your hats to hide your faces," he said. "Scarves will do just as well. I know it's hot. You little monkeys, do up those buttons. And for heaven's sake stop chewing them. Good. Are we ready to face what lies outside Monkey Land? Then off we go."

Chapter 4

Beyond the Fence

I don't mind telling you, I was more than a little bit scared as Milton Grizzlefur unlocked the main gateway and we all went under the sign that said: WELCOME TO MONKEY LAND. I even let Jem hold my paw.

We saw we were on the edge of a big town.

"Now," said Milton Grizzlefur, "we had better break up into little groups so the humans don't become suspicious.

And we'll go in different directions.
Watch out for traffic. Cars go much,
much faster outside Monkey Land. And
above all things, remember to behave
like a human. Always walk on your
back two legs. Now go. Everyone be
back here an hour before sunrise."

So we went our different ways in our
little monkey bands. Mum and Dad
gripped our paws for safety.

Milton Grizzlefur was right about the traffic. It zoomed along faster than a charging rhino.

There was so much to see. And so much that Jem and I didn't understand, and so much which had to be explained to us.

Just then, Mum was telling us about something called a lettuce box.

She said, "I've heard that humans put lettuces in that slot and post them to hungry friends —" Then she suddenly stopped. "Oh, help! Look, Otis, humans!"

"Don't panic, dear," said Dad. "It'll be all right."

Some humans went by. They looked at us strangely.

"What an ugly bunch of people," said one, when they were several steps on.

"And they must be sweltering in those heavy clothes," said another.

They turned a corner and we all burst out laughing.

"That was close," said Dad. Let's walk on the other side of the road. It's not so brightly lit."

As we were crossing the road, a dirty white van shot into view. Its horn blared. Its lights blazed.

"Look out!" screamed Mum.

We jumped for our lives. The van just missed us.

Dad went absolutely ape!

"You mad man!" he yelled. "You could have killed us." And he jumped on a fence, beat his chest and shook his head from side to side, which monkeys only do if they are seriously mad.

Mum stayed calm. "For goodness sake, Otis! Remember what Milton said. Act human!"

But it was too late. The white van
had screeched to a halt and was
reversing back.

Chapter 5

Smeelly and Fogg

Dad should never have lost his temper like that. He was sorry now. We all were.

Two humans got out of the van – one was tall, the other was short. Yet even the short one towered over us. We found that frightening. Mum and Dad huddled together with Jem and me in the middle.

The tall human was very smart. He wore a flower in his button hole. (Later, we found out his name was Bantam Fogg.)

The short one smelt like – well, not very nice. He was called Chas Smeelly.

"Well, Chas," said Bantam Fogg.

"Well, Mr Fogg," said Chas Smeelly. His hand flew out and snatched off Dad's hat. "Just as we thought, Mr Fogg. Flaming gorillas!"

"Monkeys, Chas, monkeys," corrected Bantam Fogg. "From that Monkey Land place, no doubt. But these are no ordinary monkeys, Chas. Look at them. Pretending to be humans … I expect they can understand what we say, too. You'd best open the van doors, Chas."

Chas Smeelly grinned as he opened the doors. "Doors opened, Mr Fogg," he said.

"Good." And to us Bantam Fogg said, "Listen to me, you monkey chaps. You're coming with us. There's a little job I want you to do."

And we climbed inside the van, feeling very small and very frightened.

Chapter 6

A Second Burglary

The back of the van had no windows,
so we couldn't see where we were
going. It was very bumpy. Chas Smeelly
drove fast and said a lot of bad words
about other drivers.

Then the van slowed right down. It
felt as if we were sneaking up to some
place where we shouldn't be.

Then it stopped.

Chas Smeelly turned off the engine
and Bantam Fogg looked back at us. His
smile was as friendly as a shark's.

"Now listen, you monkey chaps," he said, smiling. "I want you two big monkeys to do a job for us. Here's what I want you to do. This is Hambone Hall, a big house full of lovely expensive things. I want you to climb up and get in through the top window."

He went on. "Then I want you to start collecting up some of those lovely things. Collect as many as you can and bring them back to me and Mr Smeelly. We'll be waiting here, ready to fill our sacks."

Chas Smeelly turned around and the smell of him seemed to get stronger. "And just so you don't try any monkey business, like escaping, we'll keep the two little monkeys in the van for ..." he grinned, "... safety."

Mum looked at Dad. For the second time in one night, a spot of burglary was to be done. But this was proper burglary. Chas Smeelly and Bantam Fogg meant to keep everything for themselves.

Poor Mum and Dad. There was nothing they could do about it.

The van doors opened, and they slowly climbed out.

"We'll be back soon," said Mum. She looked so worried.

Then they were gone.

"Oh, Sandy!" wailed Jem, jumping up and down.

"Quiet in there," hissed Chas Smeelly. "Or I'll make you two into a pair of furry mittens!"

We stood up on our back legs and looked over the front seats and through the windscreen. There was a big house and Bantam Fogg was pointing up at one of its dark windows.

We saw Dad and Mum take off their shoes. Then they began to climb up a drainpipe.

After that, I couldn't bear to look.
I turned away and when I did,
I saw something that made me
whoop with joy.

"Don't do that!" said Jem, angrily.

"But, Jem. Look —"

I pointed with my paw.

"It's a key," said Jem. "Haven't keys got us into enough trouble tonight?"

"But that's not a door key," I said. "It's a key to start up the engine. I know because I've watched humans in the car park. If we can drive this thing, we can go and get help."

"And you reckon you can drive it?" Jem asked, excitedly.

"Of course!" I said, even though I wasn't really that sure.

And the next moment I was sitting in the driving seat, clutching the steering wheel with my paws, all four of them!

Chapter 7
In the Driving Seat

It was then that I found out that vans
are not made for monkeys to drive.

I couldn't see out of the windscreen.
Jem would have to give me directions.
She would also have to stand on the
pedals to make the van go or stop. I
explained to Jem how the pedals
worked.

"Brake … accelerator," she repeated.

It was crowded in the driving seat.
Jem had to stand on tiptoe and put her
head out of the side window to see.

"Ready?" I said.

"I suppose so," she said.

I turned the key.

The engine came alive. "Accelerator!"
I shouted at Jem. Suddenly we were
rushing forward. Outside, I could hear
Bantam Fogg and Chas Smeelly
snarling. Their running feet crunched
on the gravel as they chased after us.

Bam! We hit a statue and knocked off its head.

"Which way, Jem?" I hollered.

"Left!" she cried.

Baff! A different statue lost both its arms.

"Sorry, I meant right."

We clipped a tree and the main gateposts before we were back on the road. Luckily, we had left Bantam Fogg and Chas Smeelly far behind.

After a mile or two, Jem and I became much better. A team, you might say. I began to feel proud of myself. But the van must have looked very odd – as if it were driving itself!

Certainly, that was what it looked like to PC Duffle. He was parked in a side street, eating a sandwich. He shook his head. "Nah. Must be a trick of the light," he told himself, as we drove by.

Following the signs, we came in sight of Monkey Land. Jem was so excited, she forgot to say one small, important word: "Brake."

CRASH! We went right through the gates and ended up outside Mr Otterbank's house.

A light went on. A window flew open. And Mr Otterbank's head poked out.

"It's a van," he said, turning to Mrs Otterbank, who was in bed with the quilt pulled up to her chin.

"Blow me – Sandy and Jem have just climbed out. And ... and Sandy is writing something with his paw in the dirt beside the van."

"Let me see ... *HELP! Mum and Dad prisoners at Hambone Hall. Come quickly.* I'd better go and see what this is all about."

It was then that he discovered all of his clothes had gone.

"Every drawer and cupboard empty!" he wailed.

Luckily, Mrs Otterbank remembered there was something he could wear. Something Mr Otterbank had worn at a fancy dress party last New Year's Eve.

Chapter 8

Two Mean Monkeys and One Mad Gorilla

Jem and me both screamed when a
big, hairy gorilla stepped out of Mr
Otterbank's house.

"It's only me," said Mr Otterbank's
muffled voice. "Quickly, back inside the
van, both of you. No, *I'll* drive now, if
you don't mind."

He reversed the van past the
shattered gates and we were off again.

Meanwhile, PC Duffle had finished his sandwich and was eating an iced bun. "Hmm," he thought. "Isn't that the white van that looked like it didn't have a driver? I'll look more carefully this time."

And so he did.

"That's all right," he said with a sigh of relief. "There's a gorilla at the wheel … A GORILLA?"

A second later, a half-eaten iced bun was tossed aside. Blue lights flashed and a siren wailed.

I tugged at Mr Otterbank's sleeve. Mr Otterbank glanced in the mirror.

"No time to stop now, Sandy," he said, and he raced on until he reached Hambone Hall.

In the headlights, we saw Bantam Fogg and Chas Smeelly. Mum and Dad were filling open sacks with treasure from the house.

They all looked surprised when the van screeched to a halt and a gorilla sprang out, with two mean-looking monkeys on either side of him.

"Hold it right there!" cried Mr Otterbank.

"Hold it yourself," shouted Bantam Fogg, throwing a sack of treasure at him.

A big fight started: gorilla and monkeys against burglars. And then PC Duffle arrived.

He climbed out of his patrol car looking very confused.

He decided to arrest the gorilla for speeding.

But when he got him in a headlock, Mr Otterbank's mask came off.

That was too much for PC Duffle. He was so shocked that he fainted.

Outnumbered now five to two, Bantam Fogg and Chas Smeelly were quickly defeated. Mum and Dad sat on them and Mr Otterbank ran to get some rope from the van to tie them up.

"Ever been made a monkey of?" said Mr Otterbank cheerily.

Chas Smeelly used some more of his bad words. He really did know quite a few.

With the help of Mum and Dad, Mr Otterbank put Bantam Fogg and Chas Smeelly into the patrol car, with a note which read: *Arrest these two villains. They use innocent monkeys as burglars. Me and Jem put the treasure nearby for evidence.*

Mr Otterbank said, "Now, let's get out of here before that policeman comes to his senses."

Nobody had to be told twice. We jumped into the van, and Mr Otterbank drove off.

He didn't say much as he drove. It seemed like he was busy thinking.

And when he saw lots of little figures in badly-fitting shoes and clothes hurrying back to Monkey Land, he slowed down and became even more thoughtful.

He stopped outside his house and turned to Dad. "Otis," he said, "I am going back to bed. Please make sure that all the things you borrowed are left on my doorstep. And the keys, too. Goodnight."

And he went inside.

"Well," said Mum surprised. "I thought he'd be more cross than that."

Chapter 9

What Mr Otterbank
Did Next

Next morning in Monkey Land was
pretty much like any other, as far as
the visitors were concerned. But for the
monkeys there were a lot of stories to
be swapped. And everyone wondered
what Mr Otterbank would do.

Clifton Moke said he expected Mr
Otterbank would build an electric
fence.

Jem's friend, Crystal, said it was
more likely he would dig a moat and
fill it with crocodiles.

But I knew Mr Otterbank wasn't like that at all. I was right. About a week later, several big plastic bags of old clothes appeared by the tyre tree.

And on a twig was a newly cut set of keys and a note which said: *Use these wisely.*

Of course, a meeting had to be held about what this might mean. Everyone gathered at the tyre tree.

Milton Grizzlefur sat high up in his tyre, scratching himself and waiting for silence. At last he began to speak.

"Mr Otterbank is the best human who ever lived," he told us. "He realizes we are not ordinary monkeys. He knows we need to see the outside world from time to time ... And it looks like he's given us permission to do so. But listen to me, monkeys. We have to be much more careful in future."

"You can say that again," I muttered.

Later I went for a nap in my favourite tree.

"You know," I thought to myself, as I was falling asleep, "the outside world's all right, but … yawn … really, there's no place like home."

About the author

I don't like zoos or animal parks. I always feel so sorry for the animals that I want to let them out... Luckily, the monkeys in my story don't need me to do that for them. They are clever enough to get out all by themselves.

Although, now I come to think about it, the idea of meeting a monkey on a bus or in a supermarket might be rather alarming!